THE NIGHT BEFORE
CHRISTMAS
or, A Visit from St. Nicholas

The Classic Edition

by Clement C. Moore ✳ Illustrated by Charles Santore

Kennebunkport, Maine

13-Digit ISBN: 978-1-60464-033-5
10-Digit ISBN: 1-60464-033-2

Appleseed Press Book Publishers
12 Port Farm Road
Kennebunkport, Maine 04046

Design by Alicia Freile, Tango Media
Typeset in Old Claude

Printed in China
1 2 3 4 5 6 7 8 9 0
First Edition

To Major Henry Livingston, Jr.
1748–1828

C.S.

Account of a Visit from St. Nicholas

by Anonymous
as published in *The Troy Sentinel* on December 23, 1823

'Twas the night before Christmas, when all thro' the house,
Not a creature was stirring, not even a mouse;
The stockings were hung by the chimney with care,
In hopes that St. Nicholas soon would be there;

The children were nestled all snug in their beds,
While visions of sugar plums danc'd in their heads,
And Mama in her 'kerchief, and I in my cap,
Had just settled our brains for a long winter's nap—

When out on the lawn there arose such a clatter,
I sprung from the bed to see what was the matter.
Away to the window I flew like a flash,
Tore open the shutters, and threw up the sash.

The moon on the breast of the new fallen snow,
Gave the lustre of mid-day to objects below;
When, what to my wondering eyes should appear,
But a miniature sleigh, and eight tiny rein-deer,

With a little old driver, so lively and quick,
I knew in a moment it must be St. Nick.
More rapid than eagles his coursers they came,
And he whistled, and shouted, and call'd them by name:

"Now! Dasher, now! Dancer, now! Prancer, and Vixen,
"On! Comet, on! Cupid, on! Dunder and Blixem;
"To the top of the porch! to the top of the wall!
"Now dash away! dash away! dash away all!"

As dry leaves before the wild hurricane fly,
When they meet with an obstacle, mount to the sky;
So up to the house-top the coursers they flew,
With the sleigh full of Toys—and St. Nicholas too:

And then in a twinkling, I heard on the roof
The prancing and pawing of each little hoof.
As I drew in my head, and was turning around,
Down the chimney St. Nicholas came with a bound:

He was dress'd all in fur, from his head to his foot,
And his clothes were all tarnish'd with ashes and soot;
A bundle of toys was flung on his back,
And he look'd like a peddler just opening his pack:

His eyes—how they twinkled! his dimples how merry,
His cheeks were like roses, his nose like a cherry;
His droll little mouth was drawn up like a bow,
And the beard of his chin was white as the snow;

The stump of a pipe he held tight in his teeth,
And the smoke it encircled his head like a wreath.
He had a broad face, and a little round belly
That shook when he laugh'd, like a bowl full of jelly:

He was chubby and plump, a right jolly old elf,
And I laugh'd when I saw him in spite of myself;
A wink of his eye and a twist of his head
Soon gave me to know I had nothing to dread.

He spoke not a word, but went straight to his work,
And fill'd all the stockings; then turn'd with a jirk,
And laying his finger aside of his nose
And giving a nod, up the chimney he rose.

He sprung to his sleigh, to his team gave a whistle,
And away they all flew like the down of a thistle:
But I heard him exclaim, ere he drove out of sight—
Happy Christmas to all, and to all a good night.

'Twas the night before Christmas,
when all through the house,
Not a creature was stirring,
not even a mouse;

The stockings were hung by the chimney with care, In hopes that St. Nicholas soon would be there.

The children were nestled
all snug in their beds,
While visions of sugarplums
danced in their heads;

And Mama in her kerchief,
and I in my cap,
Had just settled down
for a long winter's nap—

When out on the lawn
there arose such a clatter,
I sprang from the bed
to see what was the matter.

The moon on the breast
of the new-fallen snow
Gave the luster of midday
to objects below;

Away to the window
I flew like a flash,
Tore open the shutters
and threw up the sash.

When, what to my
wondering eyes should appear,
But a miniature sleigh,
and eight tiny reindeer,

With a little old driver,
so lively and quick,
I knew in a moment
it must be St. Nick.

More rapid than eagles
his coursers they came,
And he whistled, and shouted,
and called them by name:
"Now, Dasher! Now, Dancer!
Now, Prancer and Vixen!
On, Comet! On, Cupid!
On, Donder and Blitzen!"

"To the top of the porch!
To the top of the wall!
Now dash away! Dash away!
Dash away all!"

As dry leaves that before
the wild hurricane fly,
When they meet with an
obstacle, mount to the sky,

So up to the housetop
the coursers they flew,
With the sleigh full of toys,
and St. Nicholas, too.

And then, in a twinkling,
I heard on the roof
The prancing and pawing
of each little hoof.

As I drew in my head
and was turning around,
Down the chimney
St. Nicholas came
with a bound.

He was dressed all in fur
from his head to his foot,
And his clothes were all tarnished
with ashes and soot.

A bundle of toys he
had flung on his back,
And he looked like a peddler
just opening his pack.

His eyes, how they twinkled!
His dimples, how merry!
His cheeks were like roses,
his nose like a cherry!

His droll little mouth
was drawn up like a bow,
And the beard on his chin
was as white as the snow.

The stump of a pipe
he held tight in his teeth,
And the smoke, it encircled
his head like a wreath.

He had a broad face
and a little round belly
That shook when he laughed,
like a bowl full of jelly.
He was chubby and plump,
a right jolly old elf,
And I laughed when I saw him,
in spite of myself;

A wink of his eye
and a twist of his head,
Soon gave me to know
I had nothing to dread.

He spoke not a word,
but went straight to his work,
And filled all the stockings,
then turned with a jerk,

And laying his finger
aside of his nose,
And giving a nod,
up the chimney he rose.

He sprang to his sleigh,
to his team gave a whistle,
And away they all flew
like the down of a thistle.

But I heard him exclaim,
ere he drove out of sight—
"Merry Christmas to all,
and to all a good night!"